THE HERMIT
IN ARCADIA

Also by Richard Teleky

FICTION

Winter in Hollywood

Pack Up the Moon

The Paris Years of Rosie Kamin

Goodnight, Sweetheart and Other Stories

NON-FICTION

The Dog on the Bed: A Canine Alphabet

*Hungarian Rhapsodies: Essays on Ethnicity,
Identity and Culture*

POETRY

The Hermit's Kiss

ANTHOLOGIES

The Exile Book of Canadian Dog Stories

*The Oxford Book of French-Canadian
Short Stories*

THE HERMIT IN ARCADIA

Richard Teleky

Library and Archives Canada Cataloguing in Publication

Teleky, Richard [date]
    The hermit in Arcadia / Richard Teleky.

Poems.
ISBN 978-1-55096-216-1

    I. Title.

PS8589.E375H46 2011   C811'.54   C2011-907129-0

Design and Composition by Digital ReproSet
Cover photograph by Roman Signer
Typeset in Fairfield at the Moons of Jupiter Studios
Printed by Imprimerie Gauvin

The publisher would like to acknowledge the financial assistance of
the Canada Council for the Arts and the Ontario Arts Council.

Conseil des Arts   Canada Council   ONTARIO ARTS COUNCIL
du Canada   for the Arts   CONSEIL DES ARTS DE L'ONTARIO

Printed and Bound in Canada in 2011
Published by Exile Editions Ltd.
144483 Southgate Road 14 – GD
Holstein, Ontario, N0G 2A0 Canada

Sales / Distribution:
Independent Publishers Group
814 North Franklin Street, Chicago, IL 60610 USA
www.ipgbook.com   toll free: 1 800 888 4741

For Teresa Stratas, again

CONTENTS

i

False Spring ~ *15*

Seeker ~ *16*

My Absent Friend ~ *18*

Spring ~ *19*

A Small Black Iris ~ *20*

After the Poetry Reading ~ *21*

Men Without Gardens ~ *22*

Botanical Arts ~ *23*

ii

Giverny ~ *27*

Summer, 1956 ~ *28*

At Fifteen ~ *29*

For Rennie ~ *30*

The Hermit in Arcadia ~ *31*

Inheritance ~ *37*

Linwood Park, Vermilion ~ *38*

Corpse Flower ~ *40*

iii

Translating Summer ~ 45

Clara Plays Mozart ~ 46

Night, Rain, Dogs ~ 48

Ranevskaya, at Sixty ~ 50

Gaev Replies ~ 51

Courtesans ~ 52

Sour Apples ~ 53

Listening to *Don Giovanni*: A Birthday Poem ~ 54

Listening and Watching ~ 56

Celebrities ~ 57

November 20th ~ 58

Taking the Dog Out ~ 59

Holding On ~ 60

Thanksgiving, 2007 ~ 61

Once ~ 62

In This Same Moment ~ 64

iv

Cardinals in Winter ~ 69

To Philip Larkin ~ 70

Idyll at an Untuned Piano ~ 72

Letters from X ~ 74

Chimney Sweep ~ 77

Preparing to Depart ~ 78

Plainsong ~ 79

Snow in Arcadia ~ 80

Notes and Acknowledgements ~ 83

Note on the Author ~ 85

Note on the Cover Artist ~ 86

"The hermit was *placed* in the garden exactly as one might place a pottery gnome. And there he lived out his life as a garden ornament."

—TOM STOPPARD, *Arcadia*

i

FALSE SPRING

Midnight comics tell dirty jokes,
a huckster sells new heartburn chews,
such fine sports tilt the passing hour
as you, coming closer, gather force
while lightning cracks again
beside my bed. More bulbs push up
to keep me in the yard, lingering
where time has made its peace
with wintery night, a promise
love once thought could alter life.

SEEKER

"O Röschen rot!
Der Mensch liegt in größter Not!
Der Mensch liegt in größter Pein!
Je Lieber möcht' ich im Himmel sein!"

—Des Knaben Wunderhorn

A cold February afternoon.
While sitting before the living-room window,
Mahler's 2nd in my earphones, I hear
a car speed past and a bullet
flies through the glass into the back
of my head. *O Röschen rot!* The dog
shifts in my lap, easy weight,
as blood flows in and out,
flows up and down, and my eyes
go black with the shock of pain.
No angel comes to dismiss me – none,
yet I call on neither rose nor God,
the Philharmonia continuing to thunder
a climax, an echo, another climax.
"To what purpose have you lived?"
asked Mahler. *"Lived?"* I cry.
O red red rose, you see I am
neither branch nor thorn nor flower,
but head slumped aside with a hole,
the stale bullet ache of climax and echo

over and over, waiting to flower,
the angel waiting to dismiss all
objections – a random car? – gun shot? –
chord? – calling to me incognito.

If we say no more than we can know – a harmonic
progression determines the music's ascent,
each moment's a bullet, someone has to die first –
what's left to say of death? Roses bloom,
then fade, that's the end of all loving.
O *Röschen rot*, when Mahler cried "*Gott*"
and Mozart, too, what was in the thought?

Dab blood off the sofa –
a coffin to no one –
fix yourself for the night,
feed the dog, who's been patient,
close the blinds to the fright.

MY ABSENT FRIEND

My absent friend, what your death teaches me
as I sit here alone, lost in your name,
is that absent love means bygone sanctuary.

Who wouldn't like to find space clear and free?
We tried, of course, yet dead is dead – no game.
My absent friend, what your death teaches me

beyond your absence, as far as I can see –
minutes – hours – days – now all the same,
is that absent love means bygone sanctuary.

In loss I find a new vocabulary,
words wolf down pain I cannot learn to tame.
My absent friend, what your death teaches me

once all that's left lives on as memory
of minutes – hours – days without a blame,
is that absent love means bygone sanctuary.

From loss to lost, s crashes into t
until I'm faced with only this refrain –
my absent friend, what your death teaches me
is that absent love means bygone sanctuary.

SPRING

What is it you want?
You are not clear-headed,
you drug me with scent,
lash me with colour.

But this old man clings to a rock.

A SMALL BLACK IRIS

Put a small black iris into the keyhole
in the back of a poem, open onto ice
and snow, where an abandoned
woman's dress shoe awaits discovery
by a friend, its fine black straps and
soft leather so delicate a rare old carpet
would cry out with pleasure when the sole
pressed against it, "Oh, Mother," it might
call, or "Princesse" with a French accent,
"It's time for a nightmare." But the poem
refuses sleep, finding keyholes more
than enough. "You can count on me,"
written in black ink on a scrap of
paper, flies over the drifting snow.

AFTER THE POETRY READING

You say that poems about rocks have no subject –
they're safe, you say. But rocks mean time
and nothing's safe there. Igneous isn't ignoble,
it's all that remains of long ago (oh so long ago)
when no one passed by with a camera. What
did that day sound like? Sun shone, night fell,
there might have been a morning breeze even if
no telephone rang and there were no pizzas
for delivery. What were the rocks waiting for?
If they don't deserve poems, what about flowers
or stars? Fuck the great chain of being. I will wrap
you in a lace curtain and bury your poems beside
this old rock. Let's see what happens. A poet
might fail a rock, but the rock will look back.

MEN WITHOUT GARDENS

follow blood,
rape and pillage.

This can be stopped
with an onion and a rose.

Two onions, two roses,
defy the bone-picker.

BOTANICAL ARTS

If we visit
the old glass flowers
in Cambridge, will we
come away wiser because
they have no scent?

ii

GIVERNY

While corpses piled higher in the Argonne
and bodies rotted on Vimy Ridge,
Monet surveyed his garden at Giverny,
slamming down flowers with paint,

not dissecting them – he wasn't a flatterer –
but in rapid strokes blooming a canvas
just as plant cells, light sensitive,
turned toward the sun. Ruthless,

he stomped over pollen grains,
ignored ovaries and floral sperm –
fierce activity all around him – intent on
another dab to pander perfection.

He must have watched wind pollination
because his colours moved faster than his brush:
late roses, wisteria and water lilies.
He knew without flowers the world would die.

SUMMER, 1956

You hung the sheets out on the line to dry
but they didn't billow about like angels
in some poem, they only flapped in the sun
when you came back inside to clean up Grandpa's
vomit from last night's bender, then make cookies
while I entertained you by reading aloud. I could
hear a man's voice, low, on the radio, he spoke
of "Suez" – what was that? – so I read louder
from a book with the dusty, borrowed smell
of library pleasure, and outside the sun beat
on our sheets, and upstairs Grandpa slept it off.
No one would come into our yard to steal
the laundry, and birds overhead always knew
to behave themselves. Grandma said she wasn't
married at all – it made a kind of sense, despite
their framed wedding picture. That fall, in
Budapest, your cousins would dodge bullets
like outlaws on *Gunsmoke*, but we couldn't
have guessed it as I continued to read, the next
bullet, like the next wash, an unspoken yet
assumed possibility. Of course the sheets
understood none of this. White, whiter than
sunlight, they held morning heat in their folds
and took on the soft touch of the day.

AT FIFTEEN

Struggling with my French irregular verbs
I reached out through Daudet's *Moulin*
stories to a safe time in the future
when I could speak as easily as I read
and the evening star looked really French
not only to that lonely shepherd who named
the royal constellations over the Luberon
but to me as well, the stars burning so hard,
for so long, their fires would never go out.
If I could reach back to that boy – touch
his shoulder, lead him on – would the future
have meant as much? Stars lead nowhere
                 in particular.

FOR RENNIE

To celebrate her 80th birthday, Elizabeth II
allowed a press release of essential factoids,
according to the *Times*. So far she's had
thirty corgis in her life – her favourite breed –
low to the ground like all subjects should be.
My second pug, you deserve a poem too.
I've watched you grow, grateful that the premise
of dog love worked twice. Thirty corgis mean
some after, some before, head on knee, sigh of bliss.
You would follow me through a massacre
and not just for dinner, your eyes tell me that,
those large brown eyes protruding slightly
as they observe and assess, then shine with caress.
This poem is for you, though the names
of your forbears, which helped bring it about,
make little sense to your ears; no dishonor.
We live together almost in the present,
or closer to it when you're at my side.
Gratitude's imperative, and two or thirty,
every dog deserves a share. So I succumb.

THE HERMIT IN ARCADIA

i

                    Old garage:
spider webs, dried leaves, decades of dirt
and gravel, clumps of mud, rusty nails.
And bags. Plastic stuffed into plastic,
paper folded in half, then half again.
Rope – clothesline? – and twine, a ball
of string, rolls of sticky tape. All mine.

Tool after tool, freckled with rust spots like
those livery warts called senile keratosis,
but hard – hard – yet ready to flake off
with the scratch of a thumbnail.

As I brush dried soil from a trowel, I hear
Miss Marsh – *Professor* Marsh – lecturing
that "the Romantic Movement began
when poets started to call a spade a spade
rather than an agricultural implement."
In my head for forty years, her quavering
voice led me to the library and her book
on Wordsworth. Did she have a garden?

Two doors down, Mrs. Kirk kept a garden.
Her face bitten by flowers, and snow for hair,
she lived alone through her eighties, making
beauty in iris and rose and small walks
of spiderwort. After her death a bulldozer
emptied the yard, cement was spread,
and a pole with a basketball hoop, taller
than her hollyhocks, took their place to claim
that beauty is work, just shoot baskets.

Next door, almost five decades ago,
some cancer ate Mrs. Ream's lungs
but she left behind a five-petalled rose
as pure as a medieval medallion – clear red,
like stained glass. That bush still grows
beside my fence, so every spring I rake
winter from its base and prune the deadwood.

Years, years earlier, Mrs Kolesar bent
over her dahlias, tied stems to stakes,
dead-headed offenders. She too lived alone,
tramping about in a thin housecoat
and old men's shoes, while rumor had it
that when she tended her plants, ass to street,
everyone could see she didn't wear panties.
We were cruel children, all of us, taking

her pennies at Halloween and then laughing
each summer when that story flared up again,
as bright as her dahlias, the size of that ass
requiring snickers of some kind. Of course
we never tried to smell her flowers.

iii

A rose is a prize shining
for no one, you pass by a bush
and forget to ask who once
laughed while digging its hole,
what occasion, day, choice
said, *This one, This one of all?*

iv

Now spiderwort and sex bring order
to mind as I peer at old glass flowers
painted in 1899 to match a lost specimen
of North Carolina's tradescantia rosea.
Like a boy scout from Bohemia, sweet-
faced Rudolf Blaschka spent his years
thinking of stamens and pistils and ovaries
while mixing oils to perfection, though
he'd never set foot in Southern Pines,

or anywhere in the Americas. Flowers
reproduce, say this transverse section
of an ovary, then the longitudinal slice
of seeds. Look close and you can see
a pollen grain or a portion of carola.
At home it's almost time to thin the iris,
blue as the blue flag iridacene,
model 609, painted in 1896. From
Newfoundland to Manitoba, south
to Florida and Arkansas, in marshes
and wet meadows, they once foretold
summer, until 1732, when someone
introduced them to cultivation.

v

Bees came and spoiled a corner of the garden,
cross-pollinating white phlox with dull purple
until a bleak mourning overwhelmed all,
reminding me of pointless sex. Just because
a thigh has the right curve to catch an eye,
or the cleft in an ass offers home for your hand,
there's no reason to let yourself go. Sure,
plants and people have limbs – a convention
of language – but so what? Much of each day
is accidental, like a lush, ruined garden,
though its causes can vary: lightning storm,

draught, killer ants and mould, for a start.
By now that thigh, still remembered
from years ago, will have lost its power
to take breath away. Bees didn't even play
a part, just dumb time: the garden's enemy.

vi

After the hateful end of August, then Labour Day:
the morning dew is heavier now. First, pull up
the bell-peppers – fast – so their root balls
come out clean. Does a plant feel death
enter its body? Last night's rain left the garden
wealthily wet, it's like pulling weeds from butter,
and after cutting back the day lilies I give
the phlox their final, pointless spray for fungus.
At moments like this, when a monarch butterfly
lands on a rose hip, I can't help but see the years
ahead when I won't be here to watch over the garden –
if it's a garden still and not plowed under –
years when I won't be able to pull a weed
or offer unsolicited suggestions, like Gilgamesh
calling to Enkidu, just as Grandma once called
from her bedroom window, "Don't cut my roses."

Instead of bulbs, what if October became the month
to plant an old paperback *Peyton Place* among the roses,
Out of Africa in the iris bed, a Hardy Boys adventure
beneath Grandma's peonies? I'd be glad to empty
basement bookshelves and replace compost-and-manure,
at five bucks a bag, with withering pages. Come spring,
incest and murder and tribal dances can nourish
the narcissi, which would grow taller than ever.

Although the mourning doves have been gone
for a week, and the robins even longer, I'll remain:
lone garden fixture housed for winter. But today
a modest breeze blows up and oak branches
over the garage drop acorns that plop gunfire
ping in the gutter just emptied yesterday.
Then a red squirrel runs by to bury an acorn.
These lines, buried in a book, will do for me.

INHERITANCE

Never leave a garden as a bequest,
the gift of work and trouble,
a chain to the earth, curse of bother,
hope and loss. Unless, of course,
you aim at haunting.

LINWOOD PARK, VERMILION

A boy reads *Rebecca* in an old rocking chair
    (why is he not on the beach?)
while a woman takes off her wet bathing suit,
    then cries into a pillow
as a man carries his drink — a *cold* one —
    to their screened-in porch
and ignores the reading boy and the dog,
    who lifts his head in anticipation.
The beach will be black any minute,
    thunder cracks in the distance
where the woman had said she could almost
    almost see Canada.
The CNN news-speaker chortles about
    a breaking story — people die every day —
while Mrs Danvers shows the boy and her new
    mistress some fine underwear,
since her god's in lace panties too.
    Boy reads: his habit.
    Woman cries: her habit.
    Man drinks: habit.
    Dog watches: nature.
Strictly speaking, they've all been awake
    for days and nights on end.
"There's nothing to understand,"
    thinks the woman, who wants
the black lake sky to open with fire,

explode once and for all. But
none of these people are here in the cottage,
they've all killed themselves.
Bottles gone, pillows new, well-thumbed
Rebecca book-cased for decades
now, who even remembers
the name or breed of the dog?

CORPSE FLOWER

After thirteen years, *Amorphophallus titanum* was ready
to bloom, so I stood in line, awaiting my glance

at its brief purple flowering, far from the rain forest of Sumatra,
in a Midwestern zoo. Only then did I wonder why the rare plant
was housed among animals and not in a botanical garden,

as if it might infect other valuable specimens with the stink
we were promised, giving truth to a name that should be
enough to put off anyone sensible, anyone who didn't care
to smell the stench of rotting flesh coming out of a flower.

Approaching, we knew this leper would tower over us,
a six-foot menace, and for a day or two, first in the night,
in the dark, open to the curious, not only the carrion beetle.

Soft drink in hand, I claim my place before titan arum: fresh
bruise of barbarous mauve. Now I know where I'm going.

iii

TRANSLATING SUMMER

Had Emma Bovary listened to Piaf,
and Piaf read her Flaubert,
and Flaubert not died of a stroke,
your lips might carry this weight.

Lips can turn you into something
else. Do you believe they can?
Will you agree? You've already begun
to change from knowing me.

Had Piaf regretted her lovers and
her lovers acknowledged the moon,
the moon could have let itself burn out
and this poem would cancel our doom.

CLARA PLAYS MOZART

In memoriam Clara Haskil (1895-1960)

Rococo at heart, Clara was a young Jewess
in need of escape. Half a century later, what
right do I have to write "Nazis" in a poem
so effortlessly? We've all read Celan.
Still, did Goebbels garden? We know
he listened to music, perhaps even heard
one of Clara's concerts, admired her rubato,
the way she made perfection effortless
while you waited for a mechanical moment,
some endearing flaw, but no, each phrase
threaded truth and justice and beauty together
in affront: you can be better than you are.

Bucharest born, she was that awful creature,
a child prodigy, giving concerts at five,
studying in Vienna, then Paris, suffering
in her spare time; by twenty, the lateral
curvature of her spine made a back brace
essential; next, in Marseille, she had
a brain tumour removed, before fleeing
the Nazis to Switzerland and more music,
wherever she stopped, until a December day
when she slipped and fell in a Brussels
railway station, and died of injuries.

Play the Mozart sonata in C, KV 330 —
there's nothing else like it, as if a piano
can set her free and take you along as well.
Listen: her will is turning pain into beauty,
it says, *We are here now, and I am with you.*

NIGHT, RAIN, DOGS

For Frieda Johles Forman, on Yom Kippur

      Near the Swiss border,
one late September night in 1942,
you crossed from France to freedom
of sorts, a refugee child barely five.
You still remember the barking dogs,
a sound so familiar to other refugees
it's a trope of that time. Slippery wet,
the forest floor threatened, unlike
the sidewalk where I wait tonight.

People fell, you say – especially the elderly.
The border police allowed your family
to stay, because of the children.
Did you look up at the moon, the stars?
Unlikely, I know. But if you whispered
"Let's go home" into your father's ear,
perhaps he replied, "It's all right."

Here there's rain after Indian summer,
and the foolish world's still at war
in its latest guise. Not close by yet
but war all the same. Luck, you often say,
is amoral. Is that thought in your mind
when you light the shabbos candles,
recite the shabbos prayers?

Perhaps I'm drawn to dogs because I know
only their best nature. Across the street
an old German shepherd squats to pee,
the neighbourhood Chihuahua pulls his master
along, despite its ratty dimension, and
my connoisseur pug sniffs the trunk of a tree,
rejecting its possibilities. No one is barking.

RANEVSKAYA, AT SIXTY

Dreary October rain – day after day – last night,
my darling, Mamochka's pearls had an outing – we
went to a concert – Clara Somebody-or-other,
small, who frowned – but Mozart as light as spring
breeze – you would've approved – we should have
drunk champagne afterwards, but, well, no matter,
you understand – I kept my gloves on, black cham-
ois, I can't face my hands in my lap, not any more,
and those dreadful spots, what do you call them,
tâches brunes? – for once I paid attention to the
music, all those ripples, then that sad melody in
the middle movement – and Your Friend leaned
his shoulder against mine, unnecessary, but nice –
and I started to remember hours, oh it seemed like
hours, at the old Pleyel, I was never much good
there, hadn't the least talent for it – "Just practise,"
Mamochka used to say – too long ago, my darling,
if you don't remember, who else will? – I was tired
though, so tired you can't imagine, and watching
that girl at the keyboard flattened me, really – and
I didn't want to meet anyone I knew, or talk to a
soul, Paris can be too small and I was wearing my
old coat – and I felt so useless, couldn't imagine
what to do next – you can't always – then yes, I
thought, I'll write to my brother, that's what I'll do,
tomorrow morning – so here it is –

GAEV REPLIES

Lyubichka, dear, it's raining here too, all the time! I don't listen to music any more, my ears can't take it. But yesterday I was reading a short novel by Chekhov, *Three Years* he called it. In the end, the main character, who isn't yet forty, asks, "What does the future hold for us?" Then he answers himself: "Time will tell." And *now* we know.

COURTESANS

For Eva Tihanyi

Unlike yours, my grandmother never knew
even one of the Gabor sisters, let alone two,
but it's unfair to say that only the mirrors
missed them when they left Budapest.
Courtesans don't belong just in books.
Untroubled by revolution and war,
they transcend national boundaries.
Like poets, they make us admit regret,
then count the remaining jewels.

SOUR APPLES

To hell with autumn poems,
don't offer falling leaves and cider,
fleeing birds gone wider
to a distant spring, just show me
June – June! – without a hint of death
in maturity's promise. What if
leaves never fell, apples only ripened,
birds stayed at hand? Today
I mean to write what I can't see
and see what I can write.

LISTENING TO *DON GIOVANNI*:
A BIRTHDAY POEM

Don Giovanni sings.
Don Ottavio sings.
Donna Anna sings.
Donna Elvira sings (and rants).
Zerlina sings.
Leporello sings.

Why are they singing?
(And ranting?)

One night, perhaps after dinner,
Kierkegaard observed of the opera,
"It was written only for those
who have fallen in love."
Of course Copenhagen in 1843
was a pretty bleak town,
and K. just thirty.

Sixty's the new number. Not
a number that doubles love,
it belongs to subtraction.
Kierkegaard didn't yet know
that sixty is a collision: who
cares who has fallen in love?

Still, the CD may as well sing
out with its clamouring voices,
memory's duets now safely past,
like a fading, off-stage aria.

LISTENING AND WATCHING

In the left-turn lane of the expressway
at Sheppard, Christophe Rousset plays
Rameau on a famed old harpsichord,
court dances one way to start a day.
Whichever Louis listened, I think of all
that Rameau never knew – cars and trucks,
traffic gridlock, a settled North America.
Last week I heard an upper-drawer matron
sporting a McCain button say to her double,
"I used to prefer Handel to Rameau,"
both soon to vote, discreetly, for torture.
Did they know that Handel liked to sit
naked before his London window, legs spread
and port in hand, watching the world go by?

CELEBRITIES

Today Dolly Parton visited Canada
with her new literacy project
while Parliament voted to extend
full state funerals to surviving soldiers
of the First World War. On my car radio
Dolly says she dresses like Christmas,
and I wonder why the sky's
as lurid as a cheap Christmas card,
while I remember my undergraduate
self walking home from class, Milton
under arm, memorizing a passage
from his nativity ode so long ago –
it's decades since that late November
night, crystal bright, dinner beckoning.
Here's a news flash: "Robert Altman
has died, at 81, in his Hollywood home."
A white stretch limo zooms by,
perhaps Ms. Parton's inside. Milton
can't compete now, his lines are lost.
The meaning of a season isn't clear,
forget all symbols, past and present,
turn off the radio, refuse calls of
breaking news. Somewhere in the universe
a fresh idea may want to be born.

NOVEMBER 20th

They called it a dermatological cyst,
not a tumour – *false alarm* – which
is the best we can hope for when visiting
the doctor, good nights no more,
every night we wait for mourning. What
suits you now? There's no garden
in your face, nor moon or star,
though cysts and roses share a common life.

TAKING THE DOG OUT

There are all kinds of comforts
we don't have to own – why
all this talk of property
when each new morning
gives space enough for a walk?

HOLDING ON

Permission to do what? You ask little,
more than nothing but still not enough
to know or even test. Barely, barely:
our history in your cheek, touch of breath —
a day's insecurities, you believe.

One wedding march long ago,
two children, three houses
not remembered, yet no tricks
for forgetting. You hold onto my hand,
we listen to silence, soft breathing.

A boy man from grade-school sent me
an e-mail, he spoke of "the old gang"
and I wondered what he meant,
blackmailing with the sixth grade,
fooling only himself. You hold on tighter.

Once, you told me, I walked slowly
to school as if refusing the sidewalk,
but later explained, "I love the sound
of leaves when you step on them."
Autumns later, I save the weight of your hand.

THANKSGIVING, 2007

The last time Mother died, we did it this way –
can't say anything like that, death lacking rehearsal.
Are my rights dying with you? Soon I'll sound like
those old women in the hospital elevator who,
joking together, said, "Now we only go to funerals."
"Funerals and doctors!" the taller one corrected.
Their words followed along as I walked towards
your room, words I wouldn't repeat – a new habit
I've fallen into – keeping back anything troubling,
the tubes attached to you already burden enough.
Little left to do but stroke your brow, your hand,
your swollen fingers cold in mine. Lungs full
of blood clots, another bladder infection,
pneumonia hovering, an epic catalogue of collapse
with you the warrior: Do not die on me yet.
"Accept what is," you always warned, and
with each breath I know you're leaving.
The last time Mother died, oh – *stop* –
            we did it this way.

ONCE

You took the bus along E. 105th
      to John Hay High,
            a bottle of Aspirin in your purse
in case, that day, you'd had enough
      of sleeping on a hard day-bed
            in the dining room because your sister
had married an Irish hunk
      and displaced you from the room
            you used to share with her,
weddings always causing someone grief,
      while your father's drinking flourished
            and your mother's sadness deepened.
A secretarial program, I think you took,
      with typing and business machines,
            accounting and shorthand,
some art courses, too – what happened
      to that poster you made for *The Mikado*,
            a slender Japanese girl kneeling
in her stiff orange kimono? –
      of course English and *Silas Marner*,
            the books you remembered years later
when I was reading them too,
      though I never thought to carry Aspirin
            as a safety valve. If only

I could step back in time
  to a warm spring day in 1937
    and introduce myself, your son,
as a sixty-some old man, and tell you
  about the years ahead, your long marriage,
    your joys and griefs, at least the ones
I knew of, some of which I shared.
  Perhaps knowing how things would go
    might have lessened the weight
of wanting another life of possibilities
  you couldn't dream of for yourself,
    though you gave them to your children.
All of these thoughts – and more –
  were in my head today as I drove
    past old John Hay, just renovated,
and crossed E. 105th, looking out for
  a young girl with soft brown curls,
    a girl I've seen in snapshots
and studio portraits, hand-tinted, the you
  who never took those pills
    but managed instead to hang on.
Apparently I wasn't needed then,
  life saved me for the end, when
    all I could do was bury you with love.

IN THIS SAME MOMENT

Adagio 1: a brief one

You who should have
         never did.
There is no memory
but you are here,
impress and stain.
How to say why? or
your name, in the night.

Adagio 2: the unthinkable

Turn off the alarm system
for a couple of days.

Your love life has more
to offer than you know.

Last adagio, last dance

Vous qui passez dans mes rêves
again and again,
tu es gentil.
I don't wish to embarrass
your name, in the night.

iv

CARDINALS IN WINTER

Paint-by-number is back again: the scene
out of Louisa May Alcott, two plump red birds
on bare branches before the kind of old mansion
Laurie lived in, of course snow and even
a horse-drawn sleigh reassuringly worlds away
from the Vermont teen charged with aggravated assault
for stabbing fourteen strangers with a hypodermic
found on the street. But not in this 20 x 14,
not with these acrylics (in eighteen cups),
not from that brush. The kit promises room
for true individuality, the boy sits alone
somewhere in detention, no option worth having.
What to order from this fine catalogue? Should I
send him Dutch Rum Balls or Almond Toffee?
On parole, he could dip them in poison and feed
his friends well. This morning in a faculty meeting
we're told there's a new learning curve to adulthood.
What kind of student was Laurie, or Jo March,
I ponder while walking to class, remembering
that when asked about creative writing students
Elizabeth Bishop said, "I wish they wouldn't."
Though there are no paint-by-number poems,
the young want lines to fill in safely. I dream
of passing the classroom door, pen in hand,
toward the promise of a poem's landscape,
with its plump red birds and snowy peace.

TO PHILIP LARKIN

Strange to know nothing, you wrote
at forty-four, shivering in time concrete
as air or water: *Never to be sure.*
You held on another nineteen years
with deprivation for daffodils,
a pretty thought. All lies, of course.
You had long, thin feet but no one
beautiful or devout to suck you off.
Sex did not begin in 1963, though
cold as snow your body felt it so.

Even to say you aren't *sure* begins
better than most, who fairytale themselves
with fancy. Nothing noble there. Just
sad. Sadder than the old music
left on a piano bench, or that vase
you chose as symbol in a final line.
Yes, our things last longer than we do,
a fact no faith can ever change.

You would probably not want
this reply, feted for stark grimness
as you were. Yet I can't help but think
the coming winter – your true season –

holds consolations you chose to ignore
as bad poetry, though loss and sour age,
much harder than you could say,
mock all our loves before we die away.

IDYLL AT AN UNTUNED PIANO

In memory of Nancy Walker

> *Shortly before noon, on September 26, 1945,*
> *Béla Bartók died of leukemia in West Side*
> *Hospital, New York, at the corner of Sixth Avenue*
> *and 57th Street.*

To the right of middle C, tap A.
Tap it again. The key resists
at first, untouched for a decade.
Nan once played some Bach here,
had to strike this key too, back
when piano lessons rited passage.
Neglected now, walnut lid closed,
the Krakauer stands baby grand to no
one, a *grande dame* of players already
old when the Frieds brought it home
in 1945; later, often moved, a patient
invalid. Strike a C major chord.
Alone, it echoes harshly, and I hear
more than lack of tuning – a ghost
note, sour-sweet, adagio's aftertaste.
This is the same note Bartók chose
for his last work, also in 1945.
How else to say goodbye but
a concerto for his pianist wife?
Gently, as the A strikes again,

as it turns into rain, then a chorus
of birdsong, as it circles round
itself, no longer quite present but
not detached, the sound of a man
under blood's threat. What can be
finished? Remorseless blood, rushing
at all in its path, the core of silence
interrupted once more before death,
seventeen bars left for a friend
to orchestrate; neither end nor echo.
Some praise its transparence. To me,
the still sheen of a last call known
to be final, beyond urgency, too smart
to reconcile anything with acceptance —
no, never that — a touch as light as
it must be, only thanks and regret,
for she too will follow. A makes
that clear, it must sound almost
untuned, past the ease of order,
beyond love but touched by it,
by the press of a hand that has always
known itself to be flesh, soft against
the key, softer than rain or birdsong.

LETTERS FROM X

> *"You'd be very beautiful with blonde hair."*
> *"I have blonde hair."*
> *"I know it."*
>
> —from *Hands Across the Table* (1935)

i

Now you could go there
Every inch is a branch
Let's organize something
Before the rain fever.

ii

Don't look for the best-in-show
Lou Andreas-Salomé couldn't count
Prayers and portraits bothered her
A budding poet means trouble.

iii

Born in St. Petersburg —
You have to be born somewhere —
She left for Zurich
Since everyone leaves or dies.

iv

She said, Take it slow, baby
Let's dance for a while
Be my honeybee
Until the grave opens.

v

She held his balls in her hand
They slept like candy, then wept
You can go along only so far
Then morning wants to happen.

vi

The teacher lives erotically
There's balance and then comfort
Anonymity holds great promise
As long as you can't inherit it.

vii

What are you searching for?
Too much disease makes one sick
There are beds and there are floodgates
Just listen for the hollow wind.

viii

You'll be interested in this
The butcher wants to marry me

Now let me sleep, dear
Now let me sleep.

CHIMNEY SWEEP

Not in the pages of Dickens but on my roof
this Friday morning imitating summer –
though December's in sight – you've torn
the old chimney down past its flashing,
mixed buff-coloured mortar with cement
and fine sand for new grouting that matches
the old, chosen bricks the right red
with a painter's eye. I'm tempted to climb
the ladder too but hate leaving ground,
so the new clay liners and wire caging
await pigeon eyes. When the job's done
you promise to sweep the drive clean,
though a shadow of brick dust, like ashes,
may linger awhile, or until the first snow.

PREPARING TO DEPART

I shouldn't leave you in winter
yet where I live it's longer
than spring or summer or fall,
and goodbyes rarely lullabies.

PLAINSONG

"Live now" cries the bird in a cobalt sky,
"Live now" cry the coon, the bat, the fly, but
my heart cannot hear, my head's lost in sorrow,
"All must die – you must die – I must die."

Dark moon, unbecoming, old griefs restless, reside
on a pillow beneath me, with no place to hide.
I bury my face there: "All must die – I must die."

The dog now snores soundly, his tumour benign,
a midnight breeze chills me, unbeckoned but kind,
twist and turn, we are bodies, will the next death be mine?

Make a space in your heart for the hour
of departure, cling to breath, stay the minute
as you must – night will pass. Break of day;
morning's over. See how longing can last.

Old men fall on the sidewalk, women shit in their beds,
the dog still snores contented, how much time is ahead?
No refrain can console me, rather bitter, bitter blight,
we are lost in the morning, afraid of the light.

Find a space in your heart for the thought
that life's over, learn to carry the night
like a gift overdue. Reap and sow, the sun
warns us, at end's end your death's you.

SNOW IN ARCADIA

i

The hermit catches snowflakes
on his tongue – blam! splat! plop! –
while he laughs like a fool, bitter wind
at his back. What else can go wrong?
He looks up at the sky, his nose
burning rectum-red from the cold.
"Listen, listen," he cries, but snow
continues to fall with no use for him.
A hermit belongs to the wind.

ii

The hermit's song (*all join in*):

Sing me a sad song
to help pass the night.
Buy me a bulb
for my garden's delight.
Winter is here now
and death loves a fright.

NOTES AND ACKNOWLEDGEMENTS

Many thanks to Barry Callaghan, Chris Doda, Jason Guriel, Evan Jones, Mardel DeBuhr Sanzotta, Teresa Stratas, Penelope Tzougros and Priscila Uppal, for thoughtful readings.

*****

The epigraph to *The Hermit in Arcadia* comes from Tom Stoppard's play *Arcadia* (London: Faber and Faber, 1993).

The glass flowers referred to in "Botanical Arts" and "The Hermit in Arcadia" (part iv) are in the collection of the Harvard Museum of Natural History, in Cambridge, Massachusetts.

"Ranevskaya, at Sixty" and "Gaev Replies" are based on characters in Anton Chekhov's *The Cherry Orchard*.

"Night, Rain, Dogs" was written after reading my friend Frieda Johles Forman's book, *Jewish Refugees in Switzerland During the Holocaust: A Memoir of Childhood and History* (London: Vallentine Mitchell, 2009).

Several images and references in "To Philip Larkin" come from his poems, including "Annus Mirabilis" and "Home Is so Sad."

*****

And, finally, thanks to the journals and the anthologies that originally published some of the work in the collection:

Descant – "For Rennie"

ELQ/Exile: The Literary Quarterly – "Clara Plays Mozart," "Idyll at an Untuned Piano," "Plainsong," "Ranevskaya, at Sixty" and "Seeker"

Queen's Quarterly – "Celebrities" and "Night, Rain, Dogs"

Variety Crossing – "At Fifteen" and "Men Without Gardens"

and

Crossing Lines, edited by Allan Briesmaster and Steven Michael Berzensky (Hamilton, Ont.: Serahpim Editions, 2008) – "Giverny" and "Summer, 1956"

The Best Canadian Poetry in English 2011, edited by Priscila Uppal and Molly Peacock (Toronto: Tightrope Books, 2011) – "Night, Rain, Dogs"

Richard Teleky is a Professor in the Humanities Department of York University. His books include *The Hermit's Kiss*, a collection of poems; three novels – *The Paris Years of Rosie Kamin*, which received the Ribalow Prize (U.S.) for the best novel of 1999, *Pack Up the Moon*, and *Winter in Hollywood*; a collection of short fiction, *Goodnight, Sweetheart and Other Stories*; and *Hungarian Rhapsodies: Essays on Ethnicity, Identity and Culture*; he has also edited two anthologies: *The Exile Book of Canadian Dog Stories* and *The Oxford Book of French Canadian Short Stories*. Teleky's most recent book is *The Dog on the Bed: A Canine Alphabet*, a study of representations of the human/dog bond.

Born in Appenzell, Switzerland, in 1938, Roman Signer is a leading and influential figure in contemporary European art. A visual artist known for his installations photography, video and sculpture, as well as a performance artist, he has created a unique body of work that explores the elements (earth, air, fire and water), often through collisions and explosions. For over thirty years his work has been shown in museums and galleries in Europe, North America, and Asia. The cover photograph "Water Boots" is reprinted courtesy of Mr. Signer and Hauser & Wirth, Zurich.